ANTHEM
of the FLOCK

Anthem:
A song or hymn of praise or gladness

"So we Your people
and the sheep of Your pasture
will give thanks to You forever;
to all generations we will tell of Your praise."
Psalm 79:13

ANTHEM

of the FLOCK

Life in the 23rd Psalm

———————

KELLY LARSON

Anthem of the Flock

Copyright © 2020 by Kelly Larson

ISBN: 978-1-7363482-0-8 (paperback)

ISBN: 978-1-7363482-1-5 (hardcover)

ISBN: 978-1-7363482-2-2 (eBook)

Printed in USA by 48HrBooks

(www.48HrBooks.com)

To Suzanne, my fellow sheep, who has chosen to walk this journey with me – through the pastures, the paths, and the valleys – all the way Home.

I'd like to acknowledge,
with very deep appreciation,
Laura Talbot for the amazing illustrations
&
Birda Mcleod for the "endless" revisions
and editorial counsel.

Contents

Preface

THE LORD IS MY SHEPHERD

Psalm 23 opens with one of the greatest affirmations that one could profess:

The LORD is my Shepherd!

These simple words trigger a stream of thoughts of a shepherd walking with his sheep, leading his sheep on the journey of life.

These are amazing, simple, and profound words — words that have been memorized by scores of people, old and young alike. In every nation and in every tongue where the Bible is revered, this psalm is hoisted upon the mast. They are words that have been read at funerals for comfort, for encouragement, and for security. They transcend time, geography, language, race, politics and gender.

They are beautiful words, which have launched a thousand ships of literary applause. Scores of books have been written in the attempt to mine their depths and beauty. In my own library there are many books on the 23rd Psalm, some short, some long, some new, and many as old as the nineteenth century. Some I have quoted in this book, though all have salted these pages in one way or another.

I love everything about the psalm; I am consumed by it and committed to live in it. Still, since so many volumes have been written on *this* psalm, aren't there enough on the shelves? Is there room for one more? I do hope so, and I do believe so.

But you might ask, "Of all the things that you have to write on, why would you choose Psalm 23? Isn't that a psalm that you preach on at a funeral? Isn't that something you'd find in a greeting card? Psalm 23 – isn't that a children's song that you display on a child's bedroom wall?"

I would suggest that if that's what you believe Psalm 23 is about, then you are truly missing its greatness, because the theology of Psalm 23 is as deep and as rich as *any* passage of Scripture, the depths of which are still

2

being mined. My guess is that you may know it *by heart.* How about that? I'll bet you didn't even know that you have one of the richest and deepest theological passages of the entire Bible memorized.

If you declare the Lord to be your Shepherd, if you have embraced Yahweh as your sovereign Shepherd, and if you have placed yourself in the Flock of God, then you should be (and actually *are!*) *living* in this psalm. This psalm is life, the life we have *with* God and *in* God. If we truly walk with Christ, we walk in Psalm 23 every day! Maybe you didn't know that *your* footsteps are walking through these words as well. Psalm 23 is about God's divine care over His sheep. Psalm 23 is about God's divine care over *you*!

This *song*, this *anthem*, actually outlines our spiritual pilgrimage – from the common grace that God pours over all His creation – from our initial salvation, through our triumphs and trials, to our eternal reward. This anthem celebrates the presence of God in our lives. I want to ask you. "Are you in an intimate relationship with Christ?" If you are, then you should see yourself in this very psalm; if you don't see yourself there, I fear you may be living beneath your privileges in Christ.

The LORD is my shepherd. I shall not want. He makes me lie down in green pastures. He leads me beside quiet waters. He restores my soul. He guides me in the paths of righteousness for His name's sake. Even though I walk through the valley of the shadow of death, I will fear no evil, for You are with me. Your rod and Your staff, they comfort me. You prepare a table before me in the presence of my enemies. You have anointed my head with oil. My cup overflows. Surely goodness and mercy will follow me all the days of my life, and I will dwell in the house of the LORD forever.

Psalm 23, the *Shepherd Psalm,* as it has come to be known, embodies relationship. In one word, it is about *presence*, that is, confidence in the presence of God in an individual's life. The *Shepherd Psalm* assures the believer that the divine presence attends every step of the journey.

On a grand scale this psalm heralds the covenant promise of the Good Shepherd. The author conveys thankfulness for past faithfulness, security in the present journey, and hope for the future.

What greater words of assurance could be expressed than, "The LORD is my Shepherd"?

I know of none. I know of none!

Preface

My earnest prayer and the purpose of yet another book on this cherished song is for my fellow sheep to be reminded and assured of what is theirs to gain and hold with God as their Shepherd, and to ensure that *all* would better know the great privilege it is to walk with the Good Shepherd.

The Lord is our Shepherd every step of the journey to our heavenly *Home*.

So, is there room? Is there space on the shelf for one more examination of this precious psalm? As it is all about the priceless intimacy which we enjoy every day with our Shepherd, let me exclaim, "Yes!"

In the chaos of life, we sheep can so easily forget our favored call, so we need to be reminded where we are, and who is walking with us.

Our life in step with the Good Shepherd is a glorious journey; Psalm 23 is a journal, a celebration, and an *anthem* charting those celebrated steps.

May the Good Shepherd use this volume to His glory and the encouragement of His Flock.

Kelly Larson
Bishop, California 2020

Introduction:
A Woolen Metaphor

Most people, when reciting the 23rd Psalm, would likely begin with the iconic phrase, "The Lord is my Shepherd." Altogether absent are the first two words which precede it in the Hebrew Scriptures. Yet, the superscript of this psalm tells us that it is a psalm of David.

In the Hebrew, these actual words *Mizmor leDawid,* mean *A Psalm of David* and are found in the biblical texts themselves. Though they are only advisory in many of our English translations, most Orthodox Jews as well as many Messianic Jews would ascribe divine inspiration to these words, meaning they were assigned Scriptural authority in full accordance with the subsequent texts.

The phrase *A Psalm of David* is found in some of the oldest Hebrew manuscripts, and it provides a few pieces of information to help us understand the context. There are clues yielding a time, a setting, and an author – an author who happened to be a shepherd boy – one who was to be king of Israel. It is David here in the 23rd Psalm who writes in woolen metaphor, always dually communicating the benefits of a sheep under the care of a Good Shepherd and the blessings of those who are in stride with God.

THE SETTING AND TIME
Just outside of Jerusalem, in the hills of Bethlehem, which means "the house of bread," white woolen puffs could be seen dotting the landscape. These Judean hills would in time become the location which would serve to provide the sheep for the Passover sacrifices. Nearly ten centuries before Jesus, the Lamb of God, would be birthed, one thousand years before our Good Shepherd walked upon His earth, the young shepherd David could be found among the hills caring for the flock.

THE AUTHOR
David – the future king of Israel - was the youngest of the sons of Jesse from the tribe of Judah. He would leave his mark as a musician, a writer of psalms, the slayer of Goliath, a warrior and servant of God, as well as a shepherd. Grievously, he was also an adulterer and murderer. However, at the center of it all, it was said of

him that he had a heart for God (1 Samuel 13:14; Acts 13:22).

Plain and simple, it was David who would pen this psalm under the inspiration of the Holy Spirit. This was the same David who would boldly stand before giants to defend the name of his God, and the David who would submit in defeat to his own moral failures. It is this David who would write through the lens of a sheep.

Though some moderns might claim this shepherding metaphor has become obsolete, it still remains the rich grid-work upon which we can easily observe the breadth of God's care in our lives. It clearly portrays the pure dependence that sheep have upon a benevolent Shepherd.

We can almost see a young David in the fields around Bethlehem looking after his father's sheep, recounting all the things that he does in order to protect them, in order to nurture them, in order to responsibly care for them, his leathered and weathered skin evidencing long days of labor in the sun.

Days on end he would spend away from home, walking with the sheep, watching lambs be born, rescuing some, and grieving as some died or were killed.

At this time God was preparing him for two other tasks – shepherding *people*, as well as the writing of this psalm. At some point, by the power of the Holy Spirit, David had an epiphany and was able to compare what he had done for those sheep to what God does for His people.

How often had David scouted out green pastures and restful waters? How often had he searched for the straightest paths to travel? How often had he traversed the darkest valleys, assuring the sheep that he was close by, and that he was protecting and nurturing them? How often had he kept the enemies at bay and assured his flock that they could rest in peace in his presence as their shepherd? How often had he looked for the one lost sheep who had found itself upon the rocky crag or in the thicket? How often had he played his harp to the comfort and joy of the flock? Yes, it was this seasoned David who was well-poised to pen this song.

Scripture introduces David in 1 Samuel chapter 16; he is in the fields tending sheep. Samuel, the prophet and judge, summons the young boy from the fields to anoint him as the next king of Israel.

Introduction: A Woolen Metaphor

In 1 Samuel 17, as the ruddy young lad approaches the battlefield of Goliath, he recounts his victories as a faithful and capable shepherd:

When the words which David spoke were heard, they told them to Saul, and he sent for him. David said to Saul, "Let no man's heart fail on account of him; your servant will go and fight with this Philistine." Then Saul said to David, "You are not able to go against this Philistine to fight with him; for you are but a youth while he has been a warrior from his youth." But David said to Saul, "Your servant was tending his father's sheep. When a lion or a bear came and took a lamb from the flock, I went out after him and attacked him, and rescued it from his mouth; and when he rose up against me, I seized him by his beard and struck him and killed him. Your servant has killed both the lion and the bear; and this uncircumcised Philistine will be like one of them, since he has taunted the armies of the living God." And David said, "The LORD who delivered me from the paw of the lion and from the paw of the bear, He will deliver me from the hand of this Philistine." And Saul said to David, "Go, and may the LORD be with you" (1 Samuel 17:31-37).

Quite the résumé! David recalls his own devotion as a good shepherd - the countless hours he has invested in caring for the flock of his father. Understanding the art and dedication of faithful shepherding, he pens the 55 Hebrew words which would capture the sheep's journey of life alongside the Shepherd.

This is the Anthem of Psalm 23!

Psalm 23

(Author's Translation)

A Psalm of David

Yahweh shepherds me;
I do not lack.

He makes me to lie down in tender pastures;
He leads me alongside restful waters.

He restores my soul;
He guides me in paths of righteousness
For His name's sake.

Even as I walk through the valley of deep darkness,
I will not fear any evil, for You are with me;
Your rod and Your staff comfort me.

You prepare a table before me
in the presence of my enemies;
You have anointed my head with oil;
My cup overflows.

Certainly, goodness and mercy will pursue me
all the days of my life,
So that I will dwell in the house of Yahweh, Forever!

Yahweh Shepherds

"The LORD is my shepherd, I shall not want." [1]

A SHEPHERD SHEPHERDS

From the outset David begins to weave this beautiful woolen tapestry of the Shepherd paradigm. His aim is to present the relationship between him and his Lord, between a sheep and the sovereign Shepherd of his soul. David rightly identifies Who his Shepherd is; he writes, "The LORD is my Shepherd. I shall not want." *The Lord is my Shepherd.* What familiar words! Yet if we're not careful, we fail to glean the power of those words. One of the threats of going through a Scripture that is so common is that we might say, "I've been by this so many times before. I've got it. I have it figured out already."

But as simple as that phrase may appear, it is a profound and supreme theological treatise written on the divine sovereignty of God. I want you to hear that! This is a treatise. As short as it is, it is filled with abundant theological truth. Two components need to be pointed out here: First, this is a psalm that is written by a sheep – a simple, dependent, obedient sheep; and second, David is writing a dissertation. His thesis statement is in verse one, "The LORD is my Shepherd. I shall not want." This is his overall, overarching declaration in Psalm 23.

WHAT'S IN A NAME?

This sheep's great affirmation is *"Yahweh* is my Shepherd." Many of our translations say, "The LORD." Actually, this term never existed in the original Hebrew text of Psalm 23; it would have been inserted well after David's day, though we need not be led away from our beloved translations. Devout Jews in an effort to honor the name of God chose never to pronounce *Yahweh.* In written forms they chose to insert the term *Adonai,* the Lord, in the place of God's name. Many translations use all capital letters for LORD whenever the Hebrew actually says Yahweh. But, in fairness to God, this term fails to denote the identity of the Shepherd.

But how important is it that the Hebrew says "*Yahweh*"? Actually, the letters in Hebrew are *YHWH.* This is known as the *Tetragrammaton.* It is the four-letter word (YHWH) that identifies the covenant name of God, "I AM." When God sends Moses to deliver the sons of Israel from the oppression of Egypt, Moses effectively asks God, "If they inquire, who shall I tell them sent me?" God replies, "I AM WHO I AM; Thus, you shall say to the sons of Israel, 'I AM' has sent me to you" (Exodus 3:13-14). Yahweh means "I AM"! David identifies his Shepherd as Yahweh, the Creator and Sustainer of everything, the Giver of life, who upholds all things by the Word of His power.

Let me say that once you have correctly identified Yahweh as your Savior and Shepherd, no one can do anything better for you than what God can. It is God's privilege to give you everything that you need so that you are not lacking in any good thing. Indeed, it is not a *generic* lord who is our Shepherd, but a Shepherd that is known by His name.

YAHWEH SHEPHERDS
Actually, there is even more going on in the Hebrew. The original Hebrew says simply, "*Yahweh* shepherds *me*." It is a proper noun (Yahweh) and a verb (shepherds) with a suffix (me) – only two words in Hebrew. It simply states

that Yahweh is actively engaged in the process of shepherding – it is His nature!

Now, it is relatively easy to see how translators would render this phrase "The LORD is my Shepherd," especially in light of the original wording, *Yahweh shepherds me.* I become the recipient of such shepherding actions of God. The Lord is shepherding *me!*

One author gives a description of the position of such a shepherd in relation to his sheep. In *The Shepherd Psalm,* Henry Howard writes:

> The oriental shepherd was always *ahead* of his sheep. He was down front. He was eyes and ears, heart and brain for his flock. Any attack upon them had to take him into account. He was the defense force – the advance guard that had to be measured and reckoned with. Now, what the Eastern shepherd was to his sheep, God is to his people. He is down in front, both as to time and place (Howard 1908:16).

There you go! The Eastern shepherd leads; in order to lead and defend, he walks in front of the flock rather than driving them from behind. Any attack upon the flock will have to go through the Shepherd.

That also defines the divine Shepherd. In Psalm 23, it's clear to see that *Yahweh* is privileged to perform the role of divine Shepherd as He alone can do.

SCATTERED

Certainly, God has always been the supreme Shepherd of His people throughout history, yet He has entrusted that role of shepherd to others along the way. He instructed Moses to lead His people out of Egypt. He empowered the kings, the prophets, the priests, and the judges to lead through moral, civic, and spiritual challenges. Some served well, while most did not. Ezekiel 34:5-8 communicates God's words regarding the dismal condition of the flock, when well after the time of David, trust had been considerably broken:

> *They were scattered for lack of a shepherd, and they became food for every beast of the field and were scattered. My flock wandered through all the mountains and on every high hill; My flock was scattered over all the surface of the earth, and there was no one to search or seek for them.*

Therefore, you shepherds, hear the word of the LORD: "As I live," declares the Lord GOD, "surely because My flock has become a prey, My flock has even become food for all the beasts of the field for lack of a shepherd, and My shepherds did not search for My flock, but rather the shepherds fed themselves and did not feed My flock."

The leaders of the flock of Israel had abdicated their privileged position; they had left the sheep exposed and allowed them to be scattered. In Ezekiel 34:11-12, God issues an indictment and reclaims His role as Shepherd over His flock. In time, He would gather them back again.

GATHERED

For thus says the Lord GOD, "Behold, I Myself will search for My sheep and seek them out. As a shepherd cares for his herd in the day when he is among his scattered sheep, so I will care for My sheep and will deliver them from all the places to which they were scattered on a cloudy and gloomy day."

Here in Ezekiel 34, Yahweh reasserts His authority and communicates the measure of His divine grace. He announces His divine right to take the lead as Shepherd in our lives as we step into that glorious sheepfold.

THE GOOD SHEPHERD

Ezekiel announces the prophetic words of a coming Shepherd, one from the throne of David:

> Then I will set over them one shepherd, My servant David, and he will feed them; he will feed them himself and be their shepherd. And I, the LORD, will be their God, and My servant David will be prince among them; I the LORD have spoken (Ezekiel 34:23-24).

The words "My servant David" prophesy the coming of the Messianic Shepherd Jesus, who will arrive through the Davidic line.

Progressively God reveals in Scripture the greater identity of this Shepherd; He is the *Good* Shepherd of John 10, the *Great* Shepherd of Hebrews 13, and the *Chief* Shepherd of 1 Peter 5; He is Jesus Christ. In John 10 Christ Himself appropriated this psalm to Himself in light of Ezekiel 34 — "I am the God Shepherd; the Good Shepherd lays down His life for the sheep" (John 10:11).

Of all the graces in God's good order, nothing is more precious than the presence and character of God's Good Shepherd. Our Good Shepherd is the incarnate Messiah, Jesus!

WANTS ARE NOT NEEDS

I shall not want

Unfortunately, in many of our texts, the Hebrew has been translated using the word *want*. The Hebrew literally communicates, "I do not lack," or "I lack not." It's important that we see the distinction. In my opinion, it is better translated "I do not lack" because it's not a matter of emotion. It's not a matter that *I feel* I have enough, and therefore, I don't want. If you're like me, you always want more, but the reality is that God gives us everything we *truly* need so that we do not lack. The fact that we do not lack is not bound up in want, or emotion, or identifying stockpiles of blessing; the reality of not lacking anything is a rock-solid truth.

Here is another great gem gleaned from long ago from *Lord Our Shepherd: An Exposition of the Twenty-Third Psalm* by John Stevenson:

> When the Psalmist affirms that he shall "not want," he does not mean that prosperity and abundance shall forever attend him. He makes no positive declaration of this kind. He presumes not to determine what his earthly lot shall be; but his

confidence in the pastoral care of God enables him comfortably to conclude what it shall not be, – "I shall not want." As if he had said, "Whatever may be the troubles and difficulties, the straights and changes, of my future life, I know my heavenly Shepherd will not withdraw his watchful care, nor withhold any blessing that shall be really needful for my body or for my soul!" (Stevenson 1853:56).

In the West our wants often far exceed our ability to pay for them. Our *wants* parallel our *needs* when they are placed on the same "have to have" status. If we truly believe we have everything we need and everything God desires us to have, then there should be a recognized sufficiency. It may not be in dollars, promotions, or power, but in every aspect of God's chosen providence for our lives. Surprisingly, some of our needs may be met through trials and challenges, heartbreak and loss, as well as blessing and triumph; He uses every good cross and every good favor. God uses all things for His glory to conform us to the image of Christ (Romans 8:28). He uses the good and the difficult, and it is His sovereign wisdom and right to do so.

Everything needed in this excursion of life has been abundantly supplied by the One who is able to do so. As the Shepherd seeks and gathers, as He nurtures and draws, and as the sheep then enter into His fold, the Shepherd shepherds.

Oh, that we would arrive at the point to say, "Those gifts which the Lord in His sovereignty chooses to withhold from me, I do not want to possess!"

The sovereignty of *Yahweh* and any measure of need cannot occupy the same house; they cannot exist in the same rational mind as they are opposed to one another. The Lord all-sufficiently supplies everything He sees fit to provide as Shepherd – every good mercy and every good grace to lead us *Home*.

THE GREAT DISSERTATION

With no pretensions of scholarship, this little *dissertation* portrays through the perspective of the sheep, the goodness of God through the Shepherding paradigm. The subsequent verses are drawn "directly from the shepherd's custom, and applied without interpretation to the care of man's soul by God" (Smith 1896:16).

Yahweh Shepherds

"The LORD is our Shepherd" is a great statement, yet keep in mind that "we have not the slightest right to claim this assurance, unless we have taken Christ as the guide of our life" (Miller, 1897:14).

In the pages that follow I endeavor to help us understand in greater detail the richness of the woolen metaphor.

Here in verse 1 is David's thesis statement, "*Yahweh* shepherds me, therefore I do not lack."

The Journey Begins

"He makes me lie down
in green pastures;
He leads me beside quiet waters." [2]

TRUST AND OBEY

In the verses that follow, the *author* sheep will advance the case for such fulfilled sufficiency described in verse 1. The subsequent tasks of a shepherd, those providing care and safety, are displayed in the following verses. In verses 2-6 this sheep is going to announce all of the ways in which he lacks *nothing*.

PROVISION

David begins with "He makes me lie down in green pastures. He leads me beside quiet waters."

The true shepherd would provide for His own sheep, searching the land to find adequate food and water. From the time the young ones were born, they would begin to look to the shepherd for adequate provisions. Day in, and day out, the shepherd came through. Over time the cords of trust would be developed and strengthened.

Well before dawn the flock would begin to stir, seeking their bearings as to the position of the shepherd, aligning themselves in orbit around him as another day's needs were at hand. As the flashes of first light would emerge, he would stand before the Flock, and with a familiar call bring them to the ready. Like every other day, he would lead them, and like every other day, the fleecy companions would do well to follow.

He calls. He calls. He draws them to Himself. "Those whom He has marked for His own, He will, without fail, bring Home" (MacDuff 1866:32).

The shepherd having watched over his flock by night had long before sunrise considered the day's journey. He knew the territory. Both summers and winters could be difficult times to secure food. In winter he would bring them to the tender grasses. In summer he would search out the restful waters. The faithful shepherd seldom was granted a day off. In the cool of the morning he would gather the flock together and begin the new day.

The shepherd is early astir... This is the ideal feeding time. The flock is fresh, its hunger is keen, and the pasture is moist and sweet. A shepherd always provides a full feed early in the day. It is in the consequence of their hearty eating that the sheep 'lie down.' Not in weariness, but in contentment, do they stretch themselves upon the green (Freeman 1907:25).

Invariably, there is that one sheep, that truant who in seeking to improve upon the daily fare, would head away from the fold in search of a *tastier* menu. Sheep venturing on their own can get lost or exposed to danger. But the wiser sheep, the obedient sheep, trusted the shepherd to lead them to good pastures and streams.

This verse is an affirmation of the divine provisional grace of God, an affirmation that God takes care of us at every level. Sheep are delicate creatures. May I also add that people are delicate creatures!

Though some element of rest may be present here, what is being highly communicated is the idea of being sustained. God sustains His delicate creatures. He makes them to lie down in green pastures; it is the privilege of the Shepherd to sustain life – to see to it that the sheep are led through all kinds of terrain, into places where there is moist, tender, plump green grass. When the sheep are able to dine there and are comfortable, it is then that they are able to lie down. This is the picture of satisfaction, safety, and security. They don't lie down until they are at peace. God gives them enough to eat so they can recline, they can ruminate, they can chew the cud, and they can relax.

But the Shepherd doesn't stop there, because the sheep need water as well. And so, it's the privilege of the Shepherd to lead His sheep to an area where they can get water. But sheep are skittish. They don't like going where there are rapidly moving waters, as they are prone to swim like rocks, and if their woolen coats get wet, they sink to the bottom.

The shepherd looks for calm eddies, places where water is quiet or still, where the sheep can approach, drink, and be refreshed. When calm waters are absent, the shepherd must throw rocks in the stream to dam it up and slow it down, so the sheep can be sustained.

Certainly, this verse not only speaks to material provision, but also to some element of rest for the sheep, to allow a proper rumination, perhaps to reflect upon the grace of the Shepherd; after all, a measure of trust has been gained. As well, it suggests a spiritual ingestion and a time to meditate upon the care of God, as the sheep prepare to meet the Shepherd.

Provision takes many forms and many definitions. Our wants are not necessarily our needs. In divine wisdom, our Shepherd grants to us all that He knows will be essential to the journey, and it is a great journey that awaits us!

> *But whoever drinks of the water that I will give him shall never thirst; but the water that I will give him will become in him a well of water springing up to eternal life* (John 4:14).

In verse 2, David affirms, "The Lord is my Shepherd; I lack no divine *provision*."

A Path Called "Straight"

"He restores my soul;
He guides me in the paths of righteousness
For His name's sake." [3]

RESTORED

Verse 2 describes the outpouring of God's common grace upon His creation, most notably on His sheep. But David doesn't stop there. He says, "He restores my soul. He guides me in paths of righteousness for His name's sake."

We are on the move, as David navigates into deeper truth altogether. He announces, "*Yahweh* restores my soul." What he communicates is the certainty that the soul *needs to be restored*. Augustine would echo this interpretation, that "He will *convert* my soul."

There is no small debate as to what these words imply. Is it *refreshment* to a person's spirit, or is it something that extends to the very eternal being of the soul? Does it speak to being physically revived, or does it speak to the fallen spiritual nature and lostness of a soul which has been divinely given life?

I land in the camp of the latter, though, honestly, the mechanics of such restoration are not identified. Ephesians 2:1 speaks to the deadness of a person who is lost in trespasses and sins – a person who in no way can regain true life by his or her own efforts. It is God who brings us back from death, restores us, and makes us "alive in Christ" (Ephesians 2:5).

Still, some argue a restoration of the soul spoken of here is limited to the privilege of God to turn a *backslider* back to a restored relationship with Him. I would not deny that this happens in the grace of God, but I would reason that bringing back the lost sheep is part of the journey; it is part and parcel to the "restoration of the soul."

Miller describes this restoration by saying, "The end of all Christ's restorings will be the putting back of the defaced divine image on the life of every one who trusts in him and follows him" (Miller, 1897:21).

For Christians, repentance and holiness are part of this journey as well, as the Lord continues to conform us to the image of His Son, Jesus Christ. The journey of restoration will take however long the Lord determines it needs to take. For the sheep it is a matter of trusting the Shepherd every step of the way.

For this process the words of the Lord in Psalm 19 are sweeter than honey. Psalm 19:7 promises that "The law of the Lord is perfect, *restoring* the soul," referring to the inner person - the makeup of the person. The Law of the Lord is able to restore the broken human soul. We know that the soul was broken back in Eden when Adam and Eve chose the fruit over obedience to God. It was an apostasy of the soul; communion with the Sovereign was broken.

When sin had made its wicked way into the world and into our genetic, spiritual DNA, the relationship with God - the tender, intimate relationship with God - was severed; it was *then* that the soul was broken. Men and women, made in the beautiful image of God, the *imago dei*, were damaged and no longer reflected the image with as great clarity as they had at creation.

At the point of regeneration, when a person is born again, God *begins* to restore that person to the former state of perfection, to the perfect image. "He restores my soul!"

"These words are among the most precious in this psalm. They speak to the experience of many children of God who are deeply conscious of the need of the restoring grace of the Good Shepherd" (Meyer 1895:51).

COUNTED

I will make you pass under the rod, and I will bring you into the bond of the covenant (Ezekiel 20:37).

These beautiful words of the Lord hover in the air as a promise to His people. He is the Judge over all creation and the Shepherd to watch over His chosen Flock.

The rod represents authority, as does a scepter. In this respect the rod was a symbol – an affirmation of the Shepherd's ownership of the Flock. Receiving invitation, and securing entry into the sheepfold, is granted by the authority of God through the covenant of Christ.

To "pass under the rod" did not have the same connotation as it may in modern times, as "passing under the rod" was not an act of punishment or discipline; rather, it referred to being counted and passing under the rule of the Sovereign. We can better understand the meaning of "pass under the rod" by examining its usage.

Despite the perceived simplicity of the Shepherd's life, they did have their tools of the trade. The shepherd's arsenal included his iconic staff, and his heavy woolen *abayah*, his robe, to protect him from the elements. He would also carry a gourd, or water bag, and perhaps a flute or other musical instrument to pass the time. In the shepherd's bag could be found a horn of oil to salve the wounds of the flock, and perhaps a sling and some stones. Of course, he would use the sheepfold as nocturnal quarters for the flock, and at his side would be the rod for protection and as a counting apparatus.

Yes, besides the element of weaponry, there is another, less *ferocious* aspect to this rod; the shepherd would turn it around, hold it by the *ball* end, and employ it as a *counting* tool. As he would stand at the gate, the sheep would pass by, one by one before their inspector, each one passing under the rod. "Sheep by sheep passes in review before the Good Shepherd – He knows all their cases, their circumstances, their trials, – their sorrows, their joys" (Macduff 1866:88). In a pseudo rhythmical fashion, like a ticking clock measuring the admittance of each one, the sheep would pass under it and into the sheepfold, and the tally would be taken.

THE DOOR

Christ appropriates this shepherd imagery to Himself in John 10:9, *"I am the door; if anyone enters through Me, he will be saved, and will go in and out and find pasture."*

Christ speaks of the gate, the door of entry, through which each must pass to come into His sheepfold, *the Church. The Door* references the person and work of Christ and the obedience of the sheep to enter through that Door. One by one, they enter, passing before the Good Shepherd under the rod to be inspected. A gentle tap on the back of each is the assurance that they have been duly counted among the Flock, as if to say, "This one I have purchased," and "This one is mine," and "This one is under my care." "Good to see you, friend. Come right in. You are safe, so rest easy."

All those who have entered through the Door had at one time been lost. All who have been brought into this sacred enclosure were undeservedly chosen, but now the Shepherd's unmerited grace has them covered. *"For you were continually straying like sheep, but now you have returned to the Shepherd and Guardian of your souls"* (2 Peter 2:25).

In John 10:14, Jesus speaks of Himself saying, "*I am the good shepherd, and I know My own and My own know Me.*" The Shepherd Lord knows His sheep; He inspects to see if any are limping or in need of special care. The Shepherd Lord knows how many sheep there are, if any are missing, and if any lost sheep need to be collected.

By passing through the gate to be counted, each sheep affirms the shepherd's authority and ownership - "The Lord is my Shepherd." "The Lord is my Shepherd." "The Lord is my Shepherd."

The antiphonal anthem sung by the Shepherd and the flock at sunset might be:

"The Lord is my shepherd."

"This one is mine."

"The Lord is my shepherd."

"You are safe; rest easy."

"The Lord is my shepherd."

"Come in, little one."

"The Lord is my shepherd."

"So good to see you, friend."

"The Lord is my Shepherd."

"You are counted!"

What greater joy is there than to be counted among the flock of God, the redeemed – those whom the Good Shepherd has bought for Himself with His own blood!

What greater confession do I have than "The Lord is my Shepherd!"

What greater affirmation is there than to be counted by the Lord as one of His own!

THE LOST SHEEP

The picture of the Shepherd in search of the lost sheep is clearly at the forefront here in these lines. He is a Shepherd who goes into the dark of night, along the jagged cliffs in search of the one who has made its way to danger and trial, but as MacDuff so rightly suggests, "Trial is often made the means of rousing the lethargic soul" (MacDuff 1866:208). The Shepherd desires to restore this sheep to its proper position in the flock.

David boasts, "He restores my soul." God brings us back into right alignment with Himself, and He does so by guiding us in paths of righteousness through His Word, through His will, and through His way – His *paths*. By the enlightenment of the Holy Spirit and with the clearer, fuller illumination of God's Word, He brings us to a realization of what needs to be changed in our understanding. We must understand that the initial step towards restoration comes through acceptance of Christ, obedience to Christ, and cleansing from sin in the blood of Christ. God washes His sheep in the blood of His Son in order to bring them into the Sheepfold, and into right standing before Him.

A STRAIGHT PATH

A "path of righteousness," a straight path for a sheep, is one that is safe and one with no obstacles or uncertainties. A straight path may not be the shortest distance between two points, but it "fulfil[s] the duty of paths and lead[s] to somewhere," somewhere which is known by the Shepherd (Smith 1896:17, 20). It is a path which is level and is sure to take the sheep to the desired destination. In the long run, every one of God's chosen paths leads onward to our heavenly *Home*.

What are those paths then in the journey of faith alongside the Shepherd? Paths are those directions which perfectly align to the will of God. Corporately, they are the journey by which one is brought to the correct way of redemption and atonement. These straight paths are the only way travelers will find their way to peace with their Shepherd. God as Shepherd knows the ways of righteousness and guides His sheep to that glorious end.

It seems essential to note these paths are not always gleeful, but, as will be seen in the next verse, there can be elements of gloom. Still, the sheep does not lack, as these are times to grow in faith.

FOR HIS NAME'S SAKE
David affirms that God does this for His name's sake. Do you see *why* God redeems His sheep? He doesn't do this to give glory to any one of us. He does this to exalt *Himself*.

Warner holds that "God will have special glory in the conversion of some; in the earnest work and blameless lives of others. He will help them. He will change them, for His name's sake" (Warner 1871:72-73).

There is only One who could redeem us – only One; God, by the power of His Son, redeems us. He does this for His name's sake. David is affirming that He restores me to peace with Himself.

Yes, this "teaching here has special application to the strenuous side of spiritual life... but to win that glory we must tread over long leagues of dusty road that sorely test our staying power" (Freeman 1907:64). The grade is steep for a God-nourished soul.

There are those who suggest that this verse merely refers to nourishing the flesh, or reinvigorating the body. Though it seems that God is honored with even that, He himself has set a much higher goal — the redemption of the soul.

I ask again, sheep, "Are you close at the heels of the Shepherd?"

In verse 3, David affirms, "The Lord is my Shepherd; I lack no divine *peace*."

Death Shade

*"Even though I walk through the valley
of the shadow of death,
I fear no evil, for You are with me;
Your rod and Your staff, they comfort me."* [4]

DARK DARK

In verse four, David continues on to apply this restoration to the world in which we live.

These words are a picture of what is going on in the valleys, the crevices, and the hills around Bethlehem. To get from one pasture to another requires movement from one known area to another and also through the valleys of the unknown and unsafe. There are deep crevices; it is dark at the bottom, and the sheep get nervous because they don't know what's around the corner. They are unsure what walks alongside them and how long the darkness will remain. They do not know what danger lurks.

David declares, "Though I walk through the valley of the shadow of death" (literally, "the valley of deep darkness") where things are threatening to me, "I will fear no evil, for You are with me." Ultimately, the reason he does not fear is because God is with him.

We must understand that this *death* is not referring to actual physical death, but rather threats and terror in the here and now on this journey; it is only a *shadow* of death. As we will see further on, verses 5 and 6 refer to a continuation of life here on earth which would not be possible if we were to die in verse 4!

One author writes:

> "The valley of the shadow of death" may refer to any dark, dread or awful experience through which the child of God is called to pass. In this sense it is used in many places in the Scriptures. The Christian's path is not always beside still waters and in green pastures (Evans 1921:52).

Oh! How true are those words! The valley metaphor that applies to us is in the physical realm *and* in the spiritual realm because, even though we are saved and our souls are restored, we walk through the very precarious situations of life. The course of life takes us through threatening paths, through challenges, illnesses, and defeats. In other words, faithfully walking with Christ upon the paths of righteousness does not insulate us from the wickedness of a fallen world. This valley is used as a path of righteousness, to try, to test, and to temper us.

Notably, here at the fourth verse, the level of intimacy has changed, noted by a change from the use of *He* to *You*. He's no longer talking *about* God, but *to* God. The sheep moves into a greater level of nearness to and trust in the Shepherd. God is with his sheep. *Yahweh* is with His sheep.

We must understand that this valley is simply another passage of life through which we walk alongside the Shepherd who continues leading us Home. Sometimes we may forget that though *we* walk in the dark, the Lord does not. Psalm 139:11-12 is a blessed reminder of a Shepherd unaffected by the dark:

If I say, "...Surely the darkness
will overwhelm me,
and the light around me will be night,"
even the darkness is not dark to You,
and the night is as bright as the day.
Darkness and light are alike to You.

Not only does our Shepherd *see* what lies around every turn and corner, He also sees *through* the hills, mountains, and granite boulders. He knows what evil lurks in the dark. In fact, our Shepherd knows the mind and intentions of the enemy; they are not hidden from His sight.

Evans also writes:

Is it not kind of our Father that He puts the valley in the middle of the Psalm—not at the beginning of our Christian journey, lest we should be unduly discouraged, but in the middle—after we have been strengthened with food and drink and have been assured of the tender care and guidance of the Great Shepherd. Oh! What wondrous thought and care! (Evans 1921:52).

These shadows may denote a time of distress, anxiety, remorse, or affliction, a season of spiritual warfare or darkness in others or even in our own selves. It could be physical, financial, relational, social, or even political shade that casts a pall over our spirits. These shadows describe evil, but not all evil is limited to the activities of the netherworld; rather, these shadows might include maliciousness, corruption, reputation, attack, and even general chaos.

We must remember that we are simply traversing to the other end of the valley in time, and yet we hold the presence of our Shepherd superior to any given threats to our well-being. As Spurgeon so aptly challenges us, "If you cannot trust God for the temporal, how dare you trust him for the eternal?" Not a step of this journey is wasted nor in vain, as long as we stay near the Shepherd.

And when all is said and done, I am certain we will find that the Sheep have been walking in the greater shadow of grace all along.

It is a journey of faith. Paul reminds us in Romans 8 that these times are all part of the process:

And we know that God causes all things to work together for good to those who love God, to those who are called according to His purpose. For those whom He foreknew, He also predestined to become conformed to the image of His Son, so that He would be the firstborn among many brethren (Romans 8:28-29).

If you are like me, then you have found yourself on some paths and in some valleys less traveled, some which have been unwise choices of your own making. In effect, you may be taking the lead yourself and asking the Shepherd to catch up. Yet, God says He will not abandon you. In fact, those times will still be used by His sovereign hand in His sovereign plan for your good.

A PASTORAL GOD

In rather a parenthetical way, David communicates as to why he has that kind of confident understanding, that kind of security. He says, "Your rod and Your staff, they comfort me." These two implements provide a calming assurance to the sheep and reference the authority of God as well as the nurturing nature of God.

These two implements were used back in the ancient world in order to take care of sheep. First, the rod was an implement that was fashioned from a sapling oak tree. It was cut off about 18 inches above the ground and then the root ball was harvested, effectively producing an 18-inch club. The roots were cut off, and that root ball was allowed to harden – to cure into something like a sledge hammer. The shepherd was able to use this as a club to protect the sheep. The adept shepherd had developed to the point where he could hurl this projectile at a bear, a lion, or a snake and be "dead-on" with it.

David uses this *club* metaphor to describe the authority and the power of God to be able to take care of any circumstance that might threaten one of His sheep. All forces, evil and otherwise, are checked under God's good and marshaled law. Any adversarial force lurking in the darkness is subject to God's divine authority.

In this respect the rod was a symbol and an affirmation of the Shepherd's ownership of the flock.

David continues with the staff. *"Your staff comforts me."* We've all seen it; it's the shepherd's crook. It had a hook on it and was used as a walking stick and an implement to reach into a thicket where sheep may have gotten themselves tangled. It was employed to pull sheep from the mud or from water. It was also used to pull a sheep close to the shepherd to nurture that sheep, so that it would walk closer to the shepherd.

THE VALLEY BEFORE US

We cannot avoid such valleys in life; we must walk through them. Evans cautions us of trials which lie before us, trials that we cannot avoid.

> We cannot avoid or evade passing though the valley of the shadow. We cannot dig under it, nor tunnel around it, nor fly over it. Face it we must. It behooves us, therefore, to make sure that we have the light and the life which alone will secure us for a happy exit from this valley and a glorious entrance into the glorious light of a new day…Christ the Great Shepherd will be there at the entrance to the valley to meet you and lead you through (Evans 1921:60).

In the darkness and through to the light, He is walking with us, holding us close to His side. And Christ, the Good Shepherd, has never lost a battle!

The valley must be taken head on. Sad it is for that poor sheep who is about to undertake such darkness absent of the divine Shepherd's company. But those in God's flock do not venture through alone. As God is with us, we journey with a Shepherd, His rod, and His staff. We can take comfort in both the sovereign ability of God and His nurturing nature to bless us on our journeys of faith. Every last one will make it through the valley!

In verse 4, David affirms, "The Lord is my Shepherd; I lack no divine *protection*."

Shepherd Time!

"You prepare a table before me in the presence of my enemies;
You have anointed my head with oil;
My cup overflows." [5]

D o you see the progression of the journey – from God's overwhelming love that pours out a common grace upon us, to His care for us in the physical realm, to His redemption, and then His protection from all opposition?

The progression of the journey continues with the Shepherd preparing a meal for His sheep in the midst of the enemy in order to bless them. Here in verse 5, the tone changes a bit as David reflects on the blessings of a relationship with the Shepherd. Again, as in verse 4, David is addressing the Lord directly. He says, "*You* prepare a table before me in the presence of my enemies. *You* have anointed my head with oil. My cup overflows."

Undoubtedly, this verse has been interpreted in a variety of ways, from a nomadic sheik in a tent, to a gracious palatial host, to our shepherd paradigm. However, it seems clear to me that the metaphor of shepherd is not exhausted thus far, and so the verse should be understood in light of a shepherd connecting with his flock.

A nomadic shepherd may have carried a mat, a piece of hide, or a cloth to spread on the ground as an underlayment to sleep, or a covering to eat upon as a barrier from the earth. Most likely, however, he would have employed his *abayah*, which was his Shepherd's robe – a heavy woolen robe, with a hood, and a double length of cord secured around the waist. This outer garment would have helped to warm the shepherd, and perhaps any sheep suffering severe cold, as well, could have been covered. It could have been placed upon the ground while the shepherd slept at night and served to protect him from the elements in the daytime. Likely this vestment, saturated with the scent of the shepherd, would be placed upon the ground and sat upon for brief recesses during the day.

In the context of this verse we can easily see the nearness of the sheep who have been invited to come close to the shepherd, the all too familiar scent of security wafting around the sheep.

The picture here is not that the Shepherd prepares a table in order for the sheep to dine alone, but that the sheep would partake of a meal together with the Shepherd. The snapshot here is much more than a solo picnic on a blanket in the midst of adversity; it's *Shepherd* time!

God prepares a table before me in the presence of my enemies? Now the way my mind thinks is, "Hey! Is there any place that you could prepare a table for me other than in the presence of my enemies? I've got bears around. I've got wolves around. I've got snakes. I've got bugs that want to hurt me. Along the margins are dark faces and forms, shrieks and growls, flashes and scratches, and cold. Must I have a picnic right here among these wilderness dangers? Do I have to have a meal *here*, right *here* in the open?"

The reason I believe David includes this imagery here is to emphasize that this is the kind of world we are walking in. We are the sheep. Yes, we are the sheep of

His pasture, and we are surrounded by adversaries, but until we get to glory, this is the world that we live in. They are surrounding us, seeking to lure us away from the nearness of the Shepherd.

The Shepherd sets a table of fellowship, but the enemy seeks to draw away the sheep from the safety of the Shepherd. I want to suggest that this verse is not as much about the enemies as it is about the presence of God.

In the Bible when God wanted to express intimacy or relationship with His people, what did he do? He enjoyed a meal with them.

Yahweh enjoyed intimacy and relationship with Abraham at the Oaks of Mamre (Genesis 18). He enjoyed intimacy and relationship with the elders at the base of Mount Sinai (Exodus 24). Both locations were places of covenantal relationship.

When Christ wanted to *begin* a relationship, what did He do? He invited Himself over to someone's house, and He enjoyed a meal with them. When He was building intimacy in the upper room at the last supper (Luke 22 and Matthew 26), what did He do? He enjoyed a meal with His disciples – and that forecasted a very long shadow to the *marriage supper of the Lamb,* when we will dine with the Shepherd face to face, and that ultimate intimacy will be fully realized in the heavenly realm (Revelation 19).

Christ knocks on the door and appeals, "Behold, I stand at the door and knock; if anyone hears My voice and opens the door, I will come in to him and will dine with him, and he with Me" (Revelation 3:20). Meals are a direct expression of relationship; the sort which God desires to have with us.

You see, it's about God being intimately present with us in the midst of a very difficult life, a life where we are constantly surrounded by enemies; and yet as His sheep, we are safe. The sheep are safe to enjoy intimacy with God. But don't miss it – it is also about God being with us *all* of the time!

Our lives in Christ, in the here and now, are merely an *hors d'oeuvre*; we taste a little bit of heaven before we get there – a foretaste of glory divine.

Let me ask you sheep. When was the last time you responded to the invitation to just spend time with Him? In the midst of the *tyranny of the urgent*, have you stopped to just savor Shepherd time?

COVERED

Next, the sheep says, "You have anointed my head with oil." It was the custom at the end of the shepherd's day to find a little alcove somewhere in an outcropping of rocks or trees – a sheepfold – where he would position himself at the gate as a sentry. One by one as the sheep would come in, as they would pass under the rod to be counted, the shepherd would inspect them and look at their heads for any scratches, or cuts, or bites. He would then take a homemade oil concoction, perhaps of olive oil and cedar tar, and smear it on those booboos. This concoction had an antiseptic quality, a soothing, balm-like quality. It was beautifully intimate as the shepherd inspected and cared for every aspect of each sheep.

But there's a higher level of importance to the oil. We see in the Old Testament that the symbolism of the oil is the presence of God's Spirit upon any given individual. It was a special oil made of the most precise and precious ingredients (Exodus 30:23-25). When the prophets, priests, kings, and commanders were chosen for an assignment, they would be anointed with oil, which was an affirmation that God's Spirit was with them on their journey. We see the beautiful vision of this in the

Messiah, that is, the Christ, who is the anointed One of God set apart for a very special mission.

I believe David is trying to communicate the beautiful intimacy of God's Holy Spirit with those who are counted among the flock of God. He is simply communicating, "I understand the true depth of relationship I have with you, God, and it is beautiful." The sheep appreciates the full measure of blessings that he is reaping because the Lord is his Shepherd.

MY CUP OVERFLOWS

Such are the words of the sheep David as he depicts the level of fulfillment granted by his Good Shepherd.

My cup overflows. Three simple words, and yet the imagery is profound; all of us can capture it. We can *see* it in our mind's eye – a cup, a glass, a chalice, or a goblet. Quite simply, the contents of the vessel cannot be contained. They abound and push beyond the limits; they overflow and spill over the rim. Divine measure exceeds the cup's borders.

My cup overflows. These are three simple words penned by the Psalmist, a shepherd himself who also identifies as a simple sheep journeying alongside the

Good Shepherd, enjoying abundance in divine provision, in divine peace, in divine protection, in divine presence, and in the divine promise. The psalmist is one who sees that his life is and will continue to be filled with providential favor.

My cup overflows. To my chagrin, I must confess that I often live in a world which debates a half-full/half-empty status, when no such *partially filled* vessel has ever existed. In truth, God's glorious grace continuously spills over the brim. Any such perceived deficiencies are my own contrivance. "Why can't...?" "How come...?" "When will...?" "Why not...?" The list could go on. The cup – any cup examined through the lens of these interrogations – will eventually be found parched and wanting. Yet, in the midst of those *deficits*, there is still grace - sufficient and abundant grace beyond measure.

We do well to remember that the cup of blessing from which we drink, our lives so-to-speak, were once coursing with the bitter gall of wrath, reserved for all those under the curse of sin. In His mercy the Good Shepherd drank our portion of anguish, pain, rejection, separation, and death – the guilt and the curse at the cross – and He returned to us the full portion of eternal life.

As David has affirmed in Psalm 23:1 and the Sons of Korah in Psalm 84:11, those positioned under the Shepherd lack no good thing:

> *The LORD is my shepherd,*
> *I shall not want* (Psalm 23:1).

> *For the LORD God is a sun and shield;*
> *The LORD gives grace and glory;*
> *No good thing does He withhold*
> *from those who walk uprightly* (Psalm 84:11).

Yes, so clear are the lenses of Scripture.

My cup overflows. These three simple words describe the cup of blessing – the abundance of God's favor upon all of His sheep. We do well to recognize the level of lavish kindness which saturates our lives.

My cup overflows. These three simple words are an affirmation of the sheep, that the Lord is their Shepherd, and thus, there is no lack (verse 1). The cup is a symbol of the sheep's life, a life of grace filled to over-flowing. It is not, nor ever has been, about mere happiness: it is about contentment, peace, joy, and gratitude for the grace poured out.

The cup of grace overflows with

> The grace of provision.
>
> The grace of peace.
>
> The grace of protection.
>
> The grace of presence.
>
> The grace of promise.

My cup overflows.

The cup of our salvation is a pinnacle of redemption and glory.

> *I shall lift up the cup of salvation*
> *And call upon the name of the LORD* (Psalm 116:13).

In every one of these verses, we see that the common denominator is the sheep and the presence of the Divine Shepherd; in all the situations of life, He is near.

In verse 5, David affirms, "The Lord is my Shepherd. I lack no divine *presence*."

The Journey Home

*"Surely goodness and lovingkindness
will follow me all the days of my life,
and I will dwell in the house
of the LORD forever."* [6]

LONGING TO BE HOME

The idea of *home* is a beautiful imagery. It is an arena of peace. We enjoy spending time there, and when we are not there, we long to return. It is a place of refuge and joy.

In the Christian paradigm our quest is to arrive at our heavenly Home. It is the desire to get where we have never been before, at least not in the fullest sense. Our eyes have not yet seen, and our ears have not yet heard...but someday! (I Corinthians 2:9). Our yearning is to be with and enveloped in the Lord.

Just as the sheep desire to arrive at that final destination, even more so, it is the ultimate goal of the Shepherd, to "lead 'em Home."

"Surely goodness and lovingkindness will follow me all the days of my life." I remember going to camp when I was a kid of eight years old or so. I remember singing this verse as a song and thinking that it was about some girls who were going to follow me. Shirley, Goodness, and Mercy were going to follow me all the days of my life! And yet, how errant I was!

David is communicating that there is something much grander than girls following us. You see, it's the idea of God's grace and God's mercy following us. When I read this verse in the past, I understood that grace and mercy were passively following me wherever I go. But, that's not the way God's grace and His mercy work, because they are engaged in *active* pursuit. Spurgeon tells us that God's grace and His mercy are His *footmen* to pursue us into the kingdom of heaven. Do you see that picture? They're like the faithful sheep dogs that are chasing us into the kingdom of heaven, ushering us to where we will live... forever!

PURSUED

Reminding us that the Good Shepherd is attending every step of our way, Psalm 23 briskly progresses to its beautiful crescendo of the last verse – the promise of God's *eternal* presence in our lives.

> *Surely goodness and lovingkindness*
> *will follow me all the days of my life.*

The sheep's journey, both David's journey and our journey, has been described thus far as one with the Good Shepherd always close at hand. *Goodness* is simply the best that God pictures for us in His divine mind. Even though *lovingkindness* is a word which has perhaps become a bit outdated, it speaks to the mercy of God, the overwhelming "majestic solace," and the *agape* love of God, that is, His unconditional love.

The Lord is at the helm, leading his sheep from in front, while His attending measures of favor ensure success. God's goodness and his lovingkindness, His grace and His mercy, have been bringing up the rear, for on this pilgrimage we are as much in need of His graces as we are of His forgiveness. Phillips captures this beautiful imagery, "Goodness takes care of my steps; Mercy takes care of my stumbles" (Phillips 1988:179).

These agencies of grace assure that we will *find our way Home*.

Many of our Bible translations simply use the word *follow* to describe the actions of goodness and lovingkindness on our journey, but in all truth, the word *follow* would communicate too passive a role. In fact, that word would be best translated as "chased" or even better, "pursued." The provision of God's goodness and mercy is very intentional, and they are engaged to keep us moving in obedience and in the correct direction — right on the heels of the Savior.

Goodness and mercy are divinely dispatched in order to attend, protect, and usher the sheep home, every step of the way. They are divine agencies entrusted to chaperone the believer on the journey home. They have been referred to as "The Hounds of Heaven," "Handmaidens of Heaven," and "God's Footmen." So, what are these magnificent agents of grace?

Though they are not revealed *specifically* in these brief words, may I suggest that there are various divinely appointed *escorts* for our benefit. First and foremost, I would submit that the Holy Spirit is the primary attendant of that grace and mercy. This *silent* Shepherd pursues us, convicting, convincing, assuring, guiding, and calming us, always in faithful bearing.

God also places the angelic host in service to us. "Are they not all ministering spirits, sent out to render service for the sake of those who will inherit salvation?" (Hebrews 1:14). Who is to know the number of times these angelic overseers have interceded on our behalf?

Consider the beautiful picture of Elijah as he prays for the curtain blocking the eyes of his servant's heart to be pulled back so he can see the war between good and evil taking place all around them (2 Kings 6). He hadn't seen that the angels were protecting him from harm.

The Word of God is also our escort as it influences and informs and is a light to our every step. It is "inspired by God and profitable for teaching, for reproof, for correction, and for training in righteousness, so that the man of God may be adequate, equipped for every good work" (2 Timothy 3:16-17).

Finally, God has placed *under-shepherds*, such as pastors, leaders and teachers, at the rear guard in our journeys to be signs of His divine grace and to foster our growth and faith. Yes, even fellow sheep in the flock of God encourage us.

To those whose Shepherd is Christ, this pursuit takes place in the here and now as we navigate our earthly quest, our paths of righteousness. These blessed agents are commissioned to care for us and see us to the end wherein His presence will be enjoyed forever – we will live with God for all eternity!

Psalm 139:5 and Isaiah 58:10 affirm this level of security:

You have enclosed me
behind and before,
And laid Your hand upon me.

The glory of the LORD
will be your rear guard.

He truly has us surrounded. Goodness and mercy are following us all our lives; and after that, we will live in God's house ... forever.

When David speaks of the *house*, he's not talking about the temple in Jerusalem; in fact, David is long departed before the temple is constructed. He refers instead to the "house not made with hands" mentioned in Hebrews 9:11 – the glorious, sacred space that surrounds God. He's talking about God's grace and God's mercy ushering us into the kingdom of heaven, into the presence of God. The refuge and desired dwelling place for all of God's people in all generations has been *in* God. The creation will be invited to eternally engage with the Everlasting.

THE ANTHEM'S CRESCENDO

Maybe you know the song...

> *Surely goodness and mercy*
> *shall follow me,*
> *all the days, all the days of my life.*
> *Surely goodness and mercy*
> *shall follow me,*
> *all the days, all the days of my life.*
> *And I will dwell in the house of*
> *the Lord forever.*
> *I will dine at the table set for me.*
> *Surely goodness and mercy*
> *shall follow me,*
> *all the days, all the days of my life.*
> (Peterson; 1958)

When we sing that together, it's a corporate confession of our eternal hope as the Flock of God; it's our anthem of praise! Those words are the high affirmation of our eternal future. Psalm 23:6 is a reminder of what awaits us — as His Flock! That is the grand crescendo of redemptive history.

God's fidelity to the elect is broadcast in this song. With the Good Shepherd in the lead and the attendants to the rear, we are indeed surrounded through adverse times and prosperous ones, through incredible pains and euphoric triumphs, until we arrive Home, *having been made perfect*, to stand in peace before God our Maker and our Judge... forever!

A HOUSE NOT MADE WITH HANDS

Forever is a term we often take for granted. To us in the western world it means a very long time — and then some. David doesn't use this term, but rather he employs "length of days." The idea is a strand of days without end. As our lives overflow with the presence of God, our future, forever steeped in His presence, extends for an endless chain of days. Forever!

What an incredible quest and glorious journey we are on, with the Good Shepherd leading us Home, all the way Home — to be in the presence of the Lord forever, where we were meant to be all along!

David would say, "The Lord is my Shepherd. I lack no divine *promise*."

The Sheep of His Pasture

OUR JOURNEY

Our anthem, The Shepherd Psalm, begins in an indistinct locale, and recounts our journey Home. Locations experienced along the way - pastures, waters, paths, valleys, open fields - end at a very clear and definite destination of eternal delights!

Psalm 23 comprises the lyrics of an anthem about God's faithfulness and presence in the journey of our lives. David places a divinely inspired *soundtrack* to this journey; it is *The Anthem of the Flock.*

THE SHEEPFOLD

If the Lord is truly our Shepherd, we are on the best path, resting in the best life that we could possibly enjoy right next to the Shepherd. The blessed journey begins as we step into the sheepfold of Christ through the Door; it is the entrance into the Church. The Great Shepherd has become the great sacrifice for His own Flock and has truly purchased [us] with His own blood (Acts 20:28).

Only those who have come through Jesus, who is the Door, are part of the Flock.

Only those in His Flock can claim Him as the Shepherd of their souls, and those who claim Him are advancing in holiness. As people who claim Christ as their divine Shepherd, we fail only when we settle to live below our privileges in Christ.

In this anthem David communicates so much about our journey with the Shepherd. He assures us that we can make these claims:

- The Lord is my Shepherd; I lack nothing. I have no physical needs that He cannot supply. He is my Shepherd Provider!
- The Lord is my Shepherd; I lack no spiritual needs. He is my Shepherd Redeemer. He is my Shepherd of Peace.
- The Lord is my Shepherd; I have no insecurity in times of fear. He is my Shepherd Protector.
- The Lord is my Shepherd; I have no loneliness as He envelopes me. He is the lover of my soul. He is my Shepherd of Presence.

The Sheep of His Pasture

🐑 The Lord is my Shepherd; my Home awaits me, and I lack no hope. He is my Shepherd of Promise.

My future is in eternal relationship with God *because* He is my Shepherd.

ONE WISE SHEEP
These are pretty profound words from, of all things, a sheep – a sheep who is devoted, who is submitted, who is obedient, and who has placed himself under the sovereign protective care of *Yahweh*. To those who can, and do rightly identify *Yahweh* as their Shepherd, abundant blessings are in store.

Look around and ask yourself, "What do I lack today?" If you can't say, "Nothing," you need to look again, and you need to come back to Psalm 23.

We do well to listen to the words of this wise sheep, and to receive wise counsel regarding the Good Shepherd, because every which way we turn, He has us covered.

YOU! YES, YOU!

So, who is the shepherd of your soul today? I know there are many of you today who would profess, "The Lord is my Shepherd! I do not lack." I pray that God's grace and His mercy are hounding you all the way into His glorious presence, and that you realize this.

But I'm going to guess there are some people reading these words that would say, "Kelly, I embraced the Lord as my Shepherd many years ago, but I find myself disconnected from the Flock and disconnected from God. I am that one out of a hundred sheep that is lost." I want to say that Jesus is hounding you to bring you back into the fold; He's calling you back. There's no better time than right now to come back into His fold.

But I would also guess that there is somebody reading these words, perhaps through tear-filled eyes, who may say, "I have no Shepherd. I don't know *Yahweh*. In fact, I don't even know what you're talking about."

Scripture says that "All we like sheep have gone astray. Each of us has turned to his own way" (Isaiah 53:6). You know what that's saying? It means that every individual has turned away from God. Just like sheep, we have gone astray. Each one of us has desired to live in his or her own way, to sin by eating the forbidden fruit, and to turn against the will of God. All of us! So, you are not alone.

But Scripture also says, "The Lord has caused the iniquity of us all to fall on Him" (Isaiah 53:6). You see, the reason your soul is broken is because you have not tasted of the redemption of God through the blood of Christ. God wants a relationship with you. He loves *you* so much that He sent His only begotten Son to die for sin, that if you believe in Him, you will not perish, but have everlasting life (John 3:16).

As you wear the mantle of Christ's righteousness and you allow the blood of the great "Lamb of God who takes away the sin of the world" to wash you clean, you will be able to confess, "The Lord is my Shepherd! *Yahweh Shepherds me!"*

If you're not in that camp today, there is no better day than today, right now, to turn and to enter into the Flock of God.

Anthem of the Flock

For the sheep who have. . .

- understood that they are under God's sovereign care,
- recognized that the Lord God *Yahweh* is their Shepherd,
- willfully placed themselves under the Lord's benevolent hand,
- walked that journey of life with the Great Shepherd. . .

...for *those* sheep, the journey culminates in a perpetual intimate relationship with God in the all-encompassing presence of our Shepherd.

ANYTHING BUT A SIMPLE PSALM!

Do you see what I mean? Psalm 23 is anything but a simple children's song, or a psalm we read only at funerals, or a psalm relegated to a greeting card. It's the assurance that the Good Shepherd is walking with us now and will be with us on our journey Home – all the way Home!

The Sheep of His Pasture

What a beautiful anthem the Lord gave David to pen! "On that day he gave the world this perfect lyric of religious trust, a lyric which has sung itself into the hearts of a thousand generations and will sing on until its music melts away and blends with the harmonies of Heaven" (Freeman 1907:19-20). David paints a matchless portrait of the Good Shepherd!

We truly are the sheep of His pasture. And Psalm 23 is the perennial anthem we are privileged to sing... all the way Home! Amen!

_____

*F*ather God, we thank you that we are able to come to You. What a privilege it is that You, the God of all creation, has extended an invitation to us to come into right relationship with You, into Your beautiful sheepfold.

Father, I pray that we would realize that privilege and that we would be the conquerors that You have called us to be because we are Your sheep. We pray that we could realize that Your grace and Your mercy are following us and pursuing us each and every day.

Lord, I pray for those who have become lukewarm in their relationships with You and yet find themselves washed in Your words today. Lord, I pray that they would understand the love that is before them and that You love them because You are the sovereign Shepherd.

Father, I pray for those hearts that are searching, that are confused, or that have never called you, "Shepherd." Father, I pray your Spirit would rest upon them, and convince them that You are the Way Home.

Prayer

Lord Jesus, You are the Good Shepherd that ushers us home. Thank you for these words of refreshment in Psalm 23. We thank you for glorifying Yourself. We ask that as Your church we would continue the work of ushering others Home. We give You all the glory, and we will thank You every step of the way. In Jesus precious name we pray.

And all God's sheep said... "AMEN!"

For more of Kelly Larson's writing, visit TheShepherdsPen.com

Works Cited

Evans, William. *The Shepherd Psalm.* Moody Press, Chicago, 1921.

Freeman, J.D. *Life on the Uplands.* Eaton & Mains, New York, 1907.

Howard, Henry, *The Shepherd Psalm.* Robert Culley, 1908.

MacDuff, J.R. *The Shepherd and His Flock.* James Nisbet and Company, London, 1866.

Meyer, F.B. *The Shepherd Psalm.* Hurst and Company, New York, 1895.

Miller, J.R. *By the Still Waters.* Thomas Y. Crowell Company, New York, 1897.

Peterson, John W., and Smith, Alfred B., *Surely Goodness and Mercy.* Singspiration (ASCAP) (admin. by Brentwood-Benson Music Publishing Inc), 1958.

Phillips, John. *Exploring the Psalms: Volume One—Psalms 1-88.* Loizeaux Brothers, Neptune, New Jersey, 1988.

Smith, George Adam. *Four Psalms.* Hodder and Stoughton, London, 1896.

Stevenson, John. *Lord Our Shepherd: An Exposition of the Twenty-Third Psalm.* J. H. Jackson, London, 1853.

Terrien, Samuel. *The Psalms and their Meaning for Today.* The Bobbs-Merrill Company, Inc., Indianapolis/New York, 1952.

Warner, Anna. *The Melody of the Twenty-Third Psalm.* James Nisbet & Co., London, 1871.

www.ingramcontent.com/pod-product-compliance
Lightning Source LLC
Chambersburg PA
CBHW071906020426
42331CB00010B/2692